Cache Security on ARM: Side-channel Attack and Defense

Introduction to Side-channel on ARM Platform

Naiwei Liu

Meng Yu

Ravi Sandhu

ELIVA PRESS

Naiwei Liu

Meng Yu

Ravi Sandhu

ARM platform has been in both research and industry focus for recent years. Based on its energy-efficiency, open source and security design, it is an ideal platform to develop security frameworks for mobile devices. ARM TrustZone provides secure enclaves for developers and users, helping in some secure and private execution environments.

However, just like some other platforms, ARM also has the threats of leakage private and secure information from side-channels. A side-channel is some way of getting information from collections of some types of data from the victims. Attackers collect data from energy usage, access time or even temperature change to analyze what the system might be working on. Cache on ARM devices are different from x86 platform, though both are vulnerable to side-channel attacks. This book will provide examples of FLUSH +RELOAD attack, which is one of the typical models for attackers.

We also design and implement adaptive defense framework based on side-channel threats. Our design contains both feedback and adaptive FLUSH parts, balancing performance, overhead and security. In this book, we have experiments and theoretical discussions on this framework, and both experimental and theoretical discussion results are provided in this book. This book will help future researchers develop based on our theory and the framework can be developed better in the balance of security and performance. Besides these, we calculate the performance of FLUSH operations on ARM, cost of TrustZone related operations and other performance data of instructions and operations. The data will be helpful in theoretical discussion of future design with side-channel risks.

Published: Eliva Press SRL

Address: MD-2060, bd.Cuza-Voda, 1/4, of. 21 Chişinău, Republica
Moldova Email: info@elivapress.com

Website: www.elivapress.com

ISBN: 978-1-952751-26-4

Contents

Chapter 1: On the Cost-Effectiveness of TrustZone Defense on ARM Platform

1.1 Abstract

In recent years, research efforts have been made to develop safe and secure environments for ARM platform. The ARMv8 architecture brought in security features by design. However, there are still some security problems with ARM. For example, on ARM platform, there are risks that the system is vulnerable to cache-based attacks like side-channel attacks. The success of such attacks highly depends on accurate information about the victims cache accesses. Cortex-M series, on the other hand, have some design so that the side-channel attack can be prevented, but it also needs a security design to ensure the security of the users' privacy data. In this chapter, we focus on TrustZone based approach to defend against cache-based attack on Cortex-A and Cortex-M series chips. Our experimental evaluation and theoretical analysis show the effectiveness and efficiency of FLUSH operations when entering and leaving TrustZone, which helps in design defense framework based on our research.

Keywords: ARM Platform, TrustZone, IoT Security.

1.2 Introduction

In Recent years, many research papers have been focusing on security design on ARM platform. Some of security framework are designed and implemented making use of TrustZone, a secure enclave provided by ARM on both Cortex-A and Cortex-M series. These defense frameworks target to memory protection, process protection and even cache protection. For example, some of the malicious VMs can utilize the entry/exit of the TrustZone on ARM Cortex-A, launching a cache-based attack, and compromising the message channel between victim VM and VMM. As a result, some research papers target to this problem using access control of entry/exit operations, and some papers use isolated cache protection design. The research papers and their implementations can cut down the bandwidth of cache-based attack, with various level of overhead on the whole system.

On the attacker side, many threats are threatening the IoT systems and devices. Some of them focus on systems and some of them are based on ARM chips. Cache in these devices becomes the research focus on both single device environment and cloud with multiple devices, or even IoT network connecting smart devices. The attacks can be very effective on extracting the users' private and secured data, without the permissions and access to the protected enclaves. Side-channel attack among them is a research focus. Malicious hackers can collect performance data, power consumption data or even some 'trash' data to try retrieving useful information. Attackers derive users' information like cryptographic keys, protected or private data by launching attack on the cache, and analyze the information from what they get. Some attackers just try to collect the difference in access time with different memory blocks, and predict what is accessed frequently by the users. The difference in access time can be collected if the attacker and the victims are sharing data in the cache.

ARM platform, on the other hand, is a different environment from traditional x86 structures. It has different privilege levels and sets some instructions as privileged operations. For example, cache FLUSH operation on ARM is privileged. On ARMv8-M based on Cortex-M structures, there is a much simpler structure of instructions than other platforms. This is because that ARMv8-M is designed to use in small smart devices. They have limited energy input and are asked to work in a long duration. Some of the devices are powered even by some batteries we can find in grocery stores, so the performance limitation is a thing that must be considered when designing something about security and privacy.

In this chapter, we investigate the defense effectiveness to cache based side-channel attacks on the ARM architecture. We design several tests based on TrustZone on both

ARM cortex-A and cortex-M series chips and get the performance data. These can help in design and implementation of defense, while keeping the performance and effectiveness balanced. Overall, we have following contributions in this chapter:

-- We investigate the performance overhead of TrustZone related instructions. We analyze the percentage of TrustZone instructions in real life use cases and calculate the overhead brought by these instructions;

-- We test FLUSH operation overhead and analyze clock cycles they take on different platforms. This helps in the evaluation of cost-effectiveness on both FLUSH-based attack and defense sides.

-- We provide the best/worst case of defense performance based on our experimental results and analysis.

The structure of this chapter is as follows: in Related Work section, we introduce previous research and recent research on this topic, analyzing their strong contribution and weaknesses; in Overview section, we introduce our environments of development, structure of design and security assumptions; in Implementation section, we provide some details about our design and experiment settings; in Evaluation section, we provide experimental results and discussion; and in Conclusion section we have our conclusions on the research topic.

1.3 Related Work

1.3.1 Cache-Based Attack

In a cloud computing system or a computer with multiple virtual machines (VMs), the Last Level Cache (LLC) is shared among multiple processor cores, making it vulnerable to LLC based side-channel attacks. Unlike L1 cache, LLC is much slower than L1 cache, leading to more difficult set up for side channels.

There are different ways to launch side-channel attacks, e.g., FLUSH+RELOAD [17], [6], PRIME+PROBE [6] [7] [11], and bus-locking [16]. For example, the FLUSH+RELOAD involves three steps. The attacker first flushes one or more of the desired cache contents using processor-specific instructions (e.g. clflush on x86 processors). Second, the attacker waits for sufficient time for the victim to use (or not to use) the flushed cache area. Finally, the attacker reloads previously flushed cache lines, measuring the reload time for each one of them to infer if it was touched by the victim. FLUSH+RELOAD strategy has been proven very effectively in many side channel attacks on x86 architecture. For example, Gulmezoglu et al. [6] recovered the AES key of OpenSSL within 15 seconds. Yarom and Falkner [17] recover a RSA encryption key across VMware VMs using FLUSH+RELOAD attack, and Irazoqui et al. [8] recovered AES keys using similar attack and exploiting the vulnerabilities in cache. For PRIME+PROBE attack, Work [11] recover AES keys in a cross-VM Xen 4.1 using PRIME+PROBE attack. Liu et al. [10] presented a PRIME+PROBE type side-channel attack model against the LLC, which is tested to be practical and threatens the system.

1.3.2 Hardware-Based Defense

Bernstein [2] suggested to add L1-table-lookup instruction to load an entire table in L1 cache and load a selected table entry in a constant number of CPU cycles. Page [12] investigated a partitioned cache architecture. Wang and Lee [14] [15] [13] proposed new security-aware cache designs to thwart the LLC side-channel attack with low overhead. In [15], the Partition-Locked cache (PLcache) was able to lock a sensitive cache partition into cache, and Random Permutation cache (RPcache) randomized the mapping from memory locations to cache sets. In [10], a novel random last level cache architecture that replaces demand fetch with random cache fill within a configurable neighborhood window was proposed.

While the hardware solutions provide strong isolations between the victim and the attacker, they require special hardware features that are not immediately available form commodity processors.

4

1.3.3 Software-Based Defense

Some researchers proposed to modify applications to better protect secrets from side-channel attacks. Brickell et al. [3] proposed three individual mitigation strategies: compact S-box table, frequently randomized tables, and pre-loading of relevant cache-lines. It compressed and randomized tables for AES. However, it requires manually rewriting the AES implementation and is specific to AES.

Cleemput et al. [4] applied the mitigating code transformations to eliminate or minimize key-dependent execution time variations. Crane et al. [5] proposed a software diversity technique to transform each program unique. The approach offers probabilistic protection against both online and offline side-channel attacks.

In their work, using function or basic-block level dynamic control-flow diversity along with static cache noise results in a performance slowdown of 1.76x-2.02x compared to the baseline AES encryption when using 10%-50% cache noise insertion. Dynamic cache noise at 10%-50% has significantly impact on performance (2.39-2.87x slowdown). However, above software solutions are typically application specific or incur substantial performance overhead.

1.3.4 Recent Research on ARM TrustZone

In recent years, some papers have discussions and new research findings on ARM platform, especially focusing on TrustZone protection. Zhang et al. [18] proposed an Android protection framework using TrustZone on ARM, protecting VoIP phone calls. It enclaves privacy data so the phone calls cannot be intercepted easily by malicious eavesdropping. Amacher et al. [1] have evaluate the performance of ARM TrustZone using TEEs and different benchmarks, but the security concern is out of that paper's scope. Keystone defense framework proposed by Dayeol Lee and others [9] is a good example of defense framework based on TrustZone. It enclaves protected operations and disables sharing in TLBs and memory blocks so there's no side-channel attack based on the vulnerability here.

However, the timing side-channel attack is out of that paper's scope. In our discussion, there are still risks of side-channels when exiting from TrustZone, so we need also investigate the vulnerability at the gate of security enclave.

1.4 Overview

1.4.1 Background

As multi-core processors become pervasive and the number of on-die cores increases, a key design issue facing processor architects is the security layers and policies for the on-die LLC. With LLC techniques, a CPU might only need to get around 5% data from main memory, which can improve the efficiency of CPU largely. In our implementations, we are using Intel i7-4790 processor, with 8Mb SmartCache. On ARMv8 Cortex-A platform, we are using Juno r1 Development Platform which has one A57 and one A53 processors on the board. A57 has a 2M LLC on the processor. On Cortex-M platform, we are using ARM Cortex- M4 series chips, the development platform has 3 pipeline stages and no built-in cache.

With the increasing complexity of computing systems, as well as multiple level of memory access, some registers are designed to store some specific hardware events. These registers are usually called hardware performance counters. We have many tools getting information from those performance counters, thus getting the performance information.

In our implementation, we use perf to collect the execution information of the programs. However, we cannot use perf for collecting timing information of memory access, since it cannot be accurate enough. On this chapter we use inline assemblies, e.g., rdtsc to measure time associated information with our side-channels.

1.4.2 Design on ARM Cortex-A

According to our evaluation on current on-the-market systems and applications, we find out that more and more Trusted Execution Enclave (TEE) technologies are being used on the implementations of secure system. Besides, most of the implementations are utilizing ARM TrustZone to protect the memory access and critical data. As we are interested in the performance overhead of defending using FLUSH operations on exiting TrustZone, the experiments should start from the measurements of using TrustZone, like the time cost and performance overhead.

Our experiments on ARM Cortex-A are in three different steps. For the first step, we test the cost of entering and exiting from TrustZone. After we get the exact data (clock cycles) related to TrustZone, the next step is to measure how much it takes up for the TEEs to call TrustZone related instructions or operations. On the third step, we try to clean the cache every time the system exiting from TrustZone, and see the performance overhead by these FLUSH operations added to the system. As the cache gets FLUSHed every time after the using of TrustZone, the risk of being side-channel attacked can be theoretically cut down to non-exist.

1.4.3 Design on ARM Cortex-M

Unlike ARM Cortex-A series chips, M-series chips have different structure, and with other limitations. Most IoT devices are based on Cortex-A platform, but still a rising trend that more products are using Cortex-M platform. As a result, it is still valuable to investigate the defense against malicious attackers with TrustZone. In this chapter, we have similar tests on ARMv8-M platform, measuring the performance of TrustZone, as well as FLUSH operation overhead. Our experiments on Cortex-M are using ARM Versatile V2M-MPS2 Mother- board. It offers 8Mb of single cycle SRAM, and 16Mb of PSRAM. It supports the application of different ARM Cortex-M classes, from Cortex-M0, to M3, M4, and M7. Besides these support, the development board supports simulation of ARMv8-M.

As mentioned above, on Cortex-M4 series chips, there is no built-in cache. However, the memory structure on M4 is different from other structures like x86 and Cortex-A. On that platform, memory blocks are allocated in fixed order, taking their assigned responsibilities. It is quite different from dynamic allocation, and is to the consideration of power consumption and performance overhead. Among these memory blocks, some are acting as 'cache-in-memory', so we can still see them working like cache and operate some instructions to read the working status of it.

The experiments are in two different steps. First, we measure the time cost entering and exiting from TrustZone. Next, we implement a program with TrustZone entry/exit instructions, as well as protected running steps. We then test it with controlling of the frequency of entry/exit instructions. We measure the FLUSH operation overhead according to different frequencies, and discuss the defense using FLUSH when exiting from TrustZone.

1.4.4 Threat Model and Assumptions

In this chapter, we assume that the operating system is not compromised so that the attackers are forced to use covert channels or side channels without explicitly violating access control policies enforced by the operating system or other protection mechanisms. We assume that the attacker has sufficient privilege to access the memory access time. This is also needed for the covert channel, and for the performance analysis of the covert channel.

1.5 Implementations

1.5.1 Process Structure on Cortex-A Platform

As mentioned above, the very first step for our experiment is to calculate thecost of entering and exiting from the TrustZone. On ARM Cortex-A Platform, an instruction smc is used for connecting the secure world and non-secure world. While in normal non-secure world, some code could call privileged smc instruction. Then, secure world monitor will be triggered after validation. After execution of secure code, the return of the execution also calls smc to get back to the normal world. There are many open-source test platform to measure the world switch latency, and in this experiment, we use the well-known QEMU to test. It had been developed since the first patch published in 2011, and been patched by many manufacturers including Samsung, utilizing ARM TrustZone for security design.

The process structure is show at Figure 1. When there are smc instructions trigger the TrustZone entry/exit, we trap the instructions and start using perf and other time measurement tools to calculate clock cycles they take to finish switching between trust environment and outside memory. We also FLUSH cache every time when we exit from TrustZone and see the difference in performance overhead by different frequency of TrustZone related instructions.

1.5.2 Process Structure on Cortex-M Platform

On ARM-v8 platform, SG/BXNS instructions are used to enter and exit from TrustZone. As currently almost no proper TEE for ARMv8-M is published on the market, we use a testing program instead. SG (Secure Gate) instruction is called by non-secure world code that wants to trigger TrustZone protection.

Unlike Cortex-A structure, on ARMv8-M, the page table is not used, so the memory is fully mapped with different regions. When SG instruction is called, the reserved regions for secure world are used to execute the protected part of the code. After the secure execution within TrustZone, the code has an exit called BXNS/BLXNS (Back to Non-Secure) that can lead the execution to other region besides protected ones by TrustZone. We make use of the mechanism of this, and the structure of the testing program is as Figure 2 shows.

The term cache here on ARMv8-M is part of normal memory being set as cacheable. In other words, it is a region set aside for possible cache using. On Cortex-A series chips or x86 chips, cache flush operations are just some instructions with privileges. However, the case are different on ARMv8-M. The allocation of a memory address to a cache address is defined by the designers of the applications. Because of the special structure of ARMv8-M, the cache FLUSH operations are sets of DSB (Data Synchronization Barrier) operations, with address-related instructions.

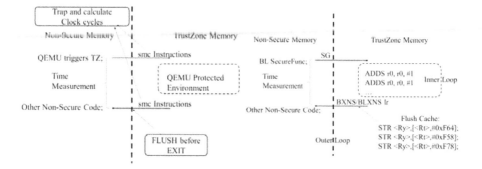

Figure 1: Process Structure on Cortex-A   Figure 2: Process Structure on Cortex-M

1.6 Evaluation

In this section, we introduce our experimental results and discussions, both on ARM Cortex-A and Cortex-M platforms.

1.6.1 Experimental Results

Cost of Entering and Exiting from TrustZone on Cortex-A. QEMU with ARM TrustZone provides us a variety of tests. The tests behave as we users initiating secure operations from user mode. The test functions validate the TrustZone features of QEMU, and utilizing the features of the functions themselves. We have tests on read/write from non-secure world to secure world and vice versa. The results are shown as Table 1 shows.

Table 1: TrustZone-Related Instruction Cost on Cortex-A

Tests	Direction	Avg. Cost (clock cycles)	Time on 800mHz
P0_nonsecure_check_register_access	Non-secure to secure	1950	2.43µs
P0_secure_check_register_access	Secure to non-secure	2200	2.75µs

Percentage of TrustZone-Related Instructions. We write a script based on the above write/read code. In the script, there is a loop called in and runs several times as a

10

workload. We use Ubuntu 16.10 as the normal world OS, with 26 processes running on background, including the workload we use for testing. We count the smc-related instructions that belongs to TrustZone-related operations, and analyze the attributions of them. According to our test, the instructions takes up less than 6% of the total instructions running, with these three different categories as shown on Table 2.

Table 2: Different Categories of TrustZone-Related Instructions

Type	Percentage
Non-secure to Secure Test R/W	2.87%
Secure to Non-secure Test R/W	2.91%
Others (Access from Background)	0.01%

In normal using conditions, however, the manufacturers are not using TrustZone that often. Thus, the test here can be the upper bound or 'worst case' of the utilization of TrustZone-Related instructions. Normally, the non-secure world does not have to call in the secure world too often.

Performance Overhead by FLUSH Operations. It is already known that ARM TrustZone on Cortex-A series are not going to clean the cache when exiting from the secure world to non-secure world. As a result, there are possibilities for the attackers to make the most of the last level cache and conduct cache-based attacks. For example, the side-channel attack of FLUSH+RELOAD, PRIME+PROBE are both found practical on the environment with TrustZone on ARM Cortex-A, some even with a fiercely high bandwidth. On the other hand, if we can FLUSH the cache every time on the 'exit' to the normal non-secure world, then it can be expected that the bandwidth of the side-channel attack can be limited to a number that is worthless to the attackers to gather the information possibly leaked by the smc operations.

We still test the performance using our test model. In this test, we are adding cache FLUSH operations on every smc instruction that calling exit from the secure world to non-secure world. On that situation, we measure the performance overhead by comparing the clock cycles of execution. At the same time, we change the percentage of TrustZone-related instructions to see the difference in the overhead. The results are shown on Figure 3 and Figure 4.

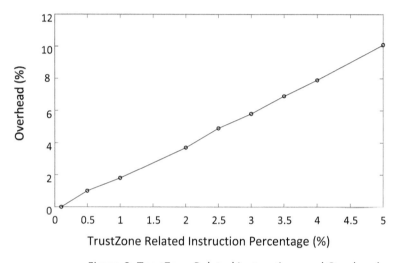

Figure 3: TrustZone Related Instructions and Overhead

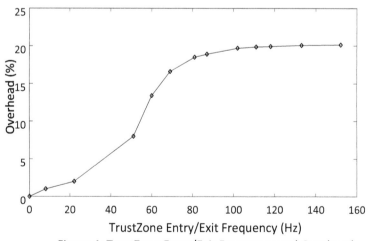

Figure 4: TrustZone Entry/Exit Frequency and Overhead

Table 3: TrustZone-Related Instructions Cost on ARMv8-M

Operation	Direction	Avg. Cost (clock cycles)
SG	Non-secure to secure	3.5
BXNS/BLXNS	Secure to non-secure	5.2

We measure the performance of the FLUSH operations using our testing program shown at Figure 2.We add FLUSH operations before executing BXNS/BLXNS operations to ensure there is nothing left when exiting from TrustZone. We measure the overhead by the FLUSH operations, and we also change the outer loop to have different frequencies of TrustZone entries and exits. The results are shown at Figure 5.

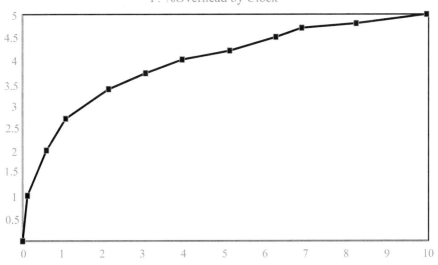

Figure 5: TrustZone Entry/Exit Frequency and FLUSH Overhead on ARMv8-M

TrustZone Usage Frequency and Flush Overhead. According to our experimental results, on ARMv8 platform, the system is connecting with TrustZone with very low frequency, taking up less than 10% of the instructions at most. Some specific instructions trigger the secure gate of TrustZone. However, when the contexts running in secured memory finish, TrustZone does not clean the cache before exit, leaving some risks here. Based on low frequency and overhead from TrustZone related instructions, we can FLUSH the cache every time when exiting from TrustZone, and still keep a low overhead of less than 20% on Cortex-A chips. This design will let the system manufacturer to put protected or private contexts into TrustZone and with no worries about side-channel attack when exiting from it.

TrustZone Discussion on Cortex-M. Unlike Cortex-A series, ARMv8-M based on Cortex-M structure is designed to have low energy cost and with much simpler system, which is thought to fit for mobile or home devices. At this case, the performance overhead brought by security protection should be controlled in a very low number. According to our experimental results, on Cortex-M structure, the secure gate instructions take much less clock cycles to execute, making it a good choice on the basis of security design. When we add FLUSH operations on exit instructions, we have even lower overhead comparing with Cortex-A chips, having less than 10% overhead at most. It is a practical design for the manufacturer to introduce and not hard to develop. On the other hand, they could put protected data and instructions into the secure enclave of TrustZone.

Cache-Based Defense on ARM Platform. Though we have no perfect way to take the place of validating cache and cleaning the TLB entries, we still have some idea for possible solutions, because there are some potential for speeding up and getting better performance. For example, we can move the FLUSH operations out from the privileged level, and try implementing another framework to ensure the security of this type of operations, while maintaining low overhead. In this chapter, we quantitatively discuss the security design for dealing with FLUSH operation requests, and there are still some more topics to research on.

1.7 Chapter Conclusions

In this chapter, we have some discussion on the effectiveness and cost of attack and defense based on ARM platform. We start from investigating the cache-based attacks. Then we design and implement some tests on ARM platform, both on ARM Cortex-A and ARMv8-M series chips. It is shown that the side-channel attack and other types of exploitations are practical and serious, causing loss to users' privacy and security. From our experimental results, TrustZone can be utilized to help defending against side-channel and covert channel attacks, but it must have an adaptive ways to manage cache operations. On the other hand, it is practical to implement FLUSH based defense on ARM platform, with reasonable overhead and good effectiveness.

In the future, we need to develop some defense framework on ARM platform, based on FLUSH operations and secure gate entry/exit instructions. The challenge will be the difference in structures of ARMv8 platform, and real-life limitations like power consumption, portable needs and other challenges. However, it is promising that ARM platform can provide the users with an environment in balance of performance, privacy, security and good mobility as well.

Chapter 2: Adaptive Noise Injection against Side-Channel Attacks on ARM Platform

2.1 Abstract

In recent years, research efforts have been made to develop safe and secure environments for ARM platform. The new ARMv8 architecture brought in security features by design. However, there are still some security problems with ARMv8. For example, on Cortex-A series, there are risks that the system is vulnerable to side-channel attacks. One major category of side-channel attacks utilizes cache memory to obtain a victim's secret information. In the cache based side-channel attacks, an attacker measures a sequence of cache operations to obtain a victim's memory access information, deriving more sensitive information. The success of such attacks highly depends on accurate information about the victim's cache accesses. In this chapter, we describe an innovative approach to defend against side-channel attack on Cortex-A series chips. We also considered the side-channel attacks in the context of using TrustZone protection on ARM. Our adaptive noise injection can significantly reduce the bandwidth of side-channel while maintaining an affordable system overhead. The proposed defense mechanisms can be used on ARM Cortex-A architecture. Our experimental evaluation and theoretical analysis show the effectiveness and efficiency of our proposed defense.

2.2 Introduction

In recent years, there is a rising trend on types of threats targeting to Internet of Things (IoT) devices. Some mobile devices based on ARM chips are also vulnerable to those threats. In the first step, some research studied the last-level cache (LLC) threats on both single device and in cloud with multiple devices [1] [2] [3] [4]. These attacks are very effective to extract users' private information without administrator's privileges. When setting up side-channel attacks, an attacker collects the information of the victim's performance, power consumption, timing, etc. The collected information can be used to further derive more information about the victim, e.g., cryptographic keys, data being accessed, and so on.

For example, memory access time can be very different depending on if the accessed data is in the cache. Thus, the data being accessed by the victim can be partially derived based on the data access time if the attacker and the victim are sharing data in the cache.

On ARM platform, a lot of research efforts have been focusing on security design and implementations. Some of security implementations [5] [6] [7] are designed and implemented using TrustZone [8], a secure enclave provided by ARM on both Cortex-A and Cortex-M series. These defense frameworks target to memory protection, process protection and even cache protection. For example [9], some of the malicious users can utilize the entry/exit of the TrustZone on ARM Cortex-A, launching a cache-based attack, and compromising the message channel between victim and host OS. As a result, some research work target at this problem using access control of entry/exit operations [6], and some research use isolated cache protection design [9]. The research papers and their implementations can cut down the bandwidth of cache-based attack, with various level of overhead on the whole system.

Defense mechanisms using hardware designs [10–14] or software modifications [15–19] have been developed to mitigate the LLC based side channel attacks on x86 environments. Though very powerful, the hardware solutions require special features that are not available on commodity computer systems. Software solutions include software diversity transform [17], adding noise into the application [18, 20, 21], isolation through better scheduling [22], and others. However, most of the solutions are application specific and incur substantial performance overhead.

However, these solutions are not perfectly set up for ARM platform. For example, when exiting from TrustZone, cache is not flushed, causing possible threats targeting to cache. On the other hand, if we plan to FLUSH cache for those TrustZone-related instructions, we must consider the balance among performance overhead, security concerns and quality of the connection through cache. However, we cannot simply port (or apply) x86 defense techniques [23] [24] [25] on ARM platform directly.

As mentioned above, LLC based side-channel attacks and defenses are mainly implemented and evaluated on the x86 architecture. While more and more mobile devices, smart phones, and IoT devices mainly use ARM architecture rather than x86. Whether the side-channel attacks and defense mechanism are the same on the ARM based devices are not fully investigated.

On the ARM architecture, it is very different to construct side-channel attacks and defense mechanisms. For example, on an ARM platform, a cache flush operation is a privileged operation. It is a more secure design than x86 since a regular user has no access to cache FLUSH operations. Furthermore, when flush instructions are requested, the system can invalidate the cache contents and FLUSH all the TLB entries, making LLC based side-channel attacks impossible, while considerable performance loss is introduced at the same time.

In this chapter, we describe an innovative approach to LLC based side-channel attacks on the ARM architecture and propose a defense mechanism for ARM Cortex-A architecture. We use adaptive FLUSH operations on some system operations, as well as the feedback of performance monitor. We carefully add cache operations to the system such that the measurement of the victim's memory access time becomes very difficult or even impossible. As a result, the bandwidth of the side channel is significantly reduced, making the attacker unable to compromise the device with an acceptable cost. We implement and evaluate the proposed defense on Cortex-A series chips. The experimental results show that our proposed defense is effective in both mitigating the cache-based side-channel attacks and supporting efficient execution of normal applications.

The design and implementation of defense have to overcome several challenges. First, on ARM architecture, there are different banked registers and modes. Flush+Reload operations are designed as privileged operations but they are supported by TrustZone in different ways. We will look at both the threat and defense in such context. Second, we target at protection of the whole system instead of a specific application while providing affordable overheads. Most existing software solutions are either specific to an application or have substantial overhead. Third, it is challenging to adaptively inject FLUSH operations with affordable overhead to the system and normal applications.

In summary, our work has the following contributions:

• We investigate the cache-based side-channel attacks on ARM architecture, with or without TrustZone protection.

• We design and implement a defense mechanism against several types of side-channel attacks on ARM platforms. The proposed defense is adaptive, effective, and efficient. The protection can work for a whole system rather than a specific application.

• We have done experimental evaluation for our protection mechanisms. The evaluation results show effectiveness and efficiency of our design.

• Our protection can be implemented in either an operation system on ARM or as a tool in more on-the-go environments.

The chapter is organized in following orders. In Related Work chapter, we introduce recent research efforts on ARM cache security and TrustZone. In Overview chapter, we have an introduction to our defense model and working mechanism. In Design and Implementation chapter, we introduce some technical details about our defense model. After that, we have sets of experiments to test the efficiency and performance of the defense. We discuss in both theoretically and experimentally in Evaluation and Discussion chapters. Then we have our conclusions and briefly plan the future work.

2.3 Related Work

2.3.1 Cache-Based Covert Channels

A covert channel can be created through sharing resources. The higher bandwidth is in the covert channel, the faster the information leakage can achieve. Ristenpart et al. [26] experimented with L2 covert channels in a cloud environment. Their bandwidth is around 0.2 bps. Xu et al. [27] extended this attack. The capacity of L2 cover channel is 233 bps. Percival demonstrated that shared access to memory caches provides a high bandwidth covert channel between threads in [28]. The capacity of L2 covert channel is approximately 100 kbps. Wu et al. [29] presented a new covert channel attack with high-bandwidth (over 190.4 kbps) and reliable data transmission in the cloud. Liu et al. presented a Prime+Probe side-channel attack, achieving a bandwidth of 1.2 mbps [19].

By accurately mapping the cache sets, our attack achieves a much higher bandwidth than prior work.

2.3.2 Last-level Cache (LLC) Side-Channel Attacks

Due to the low channel capacity, an LLC-based side-channel typically only leaks course-grain information. For example, the attacks of Ristenpart et al. [26] leak information about co-residency, traffic rates and keystroke timing. Zhang et al. [30] use an L2 side-channel to detect non-cooperating co-resident VMs. Our attack improves on this work by achieving a high granularity that enables leaking of cryptographic keys. Yarom and Falkner (FLUSH+RELOAD) [1] show that when attacker and victim share memory, e.g. shared libraries, the technique of Gullasch et al. [31] can achieve an efficient crossVM, cross-core, LLC attack. Side-channel attack removes the requirement for sharing memory, and is powerful enough to recover the key from the latest GnuPG crypto software which uses the more advanced 618 sliding window technique for modular exponentiation, which is impossible using FLUSH+RELOAD attacks. In concurrent work Irazoqui et al. [32] describe the use of large pages for mounting a synchronous LLC PRIME+PROBE attack against the last round of AES.

Recently, many research work on side-channel attacks in a Trusted Execution Environment (TEE), such as Intel SGX and ARM Trustzone [33, 34]. There are some other types of side-channel attacks based on different shared data or data structures in the system. For example, Xu et al. [35] introduced controlled-channel attacks, a new type of side-channel attack. The attack allows an untrusted operating system to extract large amounts of sensitive information from protected applications on systems, such as Overshadow [36], InkTag [37], or Haven [38]. This attack is not based on LLC, but based on the page accessed by the VMs. Our techniques do not apply directly to these attacks but the idea of noise injection can still be used theoretically.

Basically, the difference between a covert channel and a side-channel is the role of the attacker side. In a covert channel, the attacker trying to get the encrypted message can be either side of the channel, possibly the sender or the receiver. However, in a side-channel, the attacker is on a third side, trying to listen to the message channel to steal information. Both the sender and the receiver can be unaware of the existence of the malicious user.

2.3.3 Manipulating Cache Contents

Two types of LLC-based side-channels have been extensively studied recently. One is the Flush+Reload [1–4], and the other is Prime+Probe [4, 19, 32]. In Flush+Reload, the attacker and victim share a physical memory page, such as sharing libraries. In [30], the adversary was able to conduct a cache-based attack to track the execution path of a victim and extract a secret of interest from the victim. Yarom and Falkner [1] applied the attack to recover an RSA encryption key across VMware VMs, and Irazoqui et al. [2] recovered AES keys. Prime+Probe can be conducted when the attacker and victim share the same CPU cache sets. Liu et al. presented an effective and practical implementation of the Prime+Probe side-channel attack against the last-level cache in [19]. Work [32] implemented Prime+Probe to recover AES keys in a cross-VM setting on Xen 4.1.

It is proven that the Flush+Reload technique is particularly effective when memory duplication features are enabled by the VMM [2, 4]. Gülmezoglu et al. applied Flush+Reload attack on OpenSSL implementation of AES, and recovered the key in just 15 seconds working across cores in a cross-VM setting [4]. In this chapter, we mainly focus on Flush+Reload technique and our proposed techniques can also be applied to Prime+Probe using the same principle.

The FLUSH and RELOAD technique is a variant of Prime+Probe that relies on sharing pages between the attacker and the victim processes. With shared pages, the malicious user can ensure that a specific memory line is evicted from the whole cache hierarchy. The attacker uses this to monitor access to the memory line. The attack is a variation of the technique suggested by Gullasch et al. [31], which include adaptations to multi-core and virtualized environments.

A round of attack consists of three phases. During the first phase, the monitored memory line is flushed from the cache hierarchy. The attacker, then, waits to allow the victim time to access the memory line before the third phase. In the third phase, the attacker reloads the memory line, measuring the time to load it. If during the wait phase the victim accesses the memory line, the line will be available in the cache and the reload operation will take a short time. If, on the other hand, the victim has not accessed the memory line, the line will need to be brought from memory and the reload will take significantly longer.

The victim access can overlap the reload phase of the attacker. In such a case, the victim access will not trigger a cache fill. Instead, the victim will use the cached data from the reload phase. Consequently, the attacker will miss the access.

2.3.4 Noise Injection based Defense

Page [20] suggested manually adding noise, such as garbage instructions, and random loads, into the encryption routine to make cache side-channel attacks more difficult. The proposed approach is specific to encryption application and incurs substantial performance overhead. Tromer et al. [18] suggested several countermeasures for the side channel attack, including injecting noise to the memory access pattern by adding spurious accesses, e.g., by performing a dummy encryption in parallel to the real one. This would decrease the signal visible to the attacker. However, they do not give any detailed design or implementation.

Zhang and Reiter [21] designed and implemented a defense system called Düppel that enables a tenant virtual machine to defend itself from cache-based side-channel attacks in public clouds. A tenant can automatically inject additional noise into the timings that an attacker might observe from caches. Since these timings are commonly used by an attacker to infer the sensitive information about a victim VM, injecting noise into them will generally make the attacks more difficult. The solution requires users to identify the particular processes that should be protected [39]. Our approach generally protects the system and does not need user to identify any specific process.

2.3.5 Other Types of Defense

Zhou et al. [39] proposed a memory copy approach to dynamically manage physical memory pages shared between security domains to disable sharing of LLC lines, preventing Flush+Reload side channels via LLCs. In their proposed work, a victim's access to its copy will be invisible to an attacker's Reload in a Flush+Reload attack. Varadarajan et al. [22] investigated a soft isolation, reducing the risk of sharing through better scheduling design. It is also possible to limit the frequency of potentially dangerous interactions between mutually untrustworthy programs [40].

Compared with the above work, our approach is easy to deploy and effective, and provides protection to an entire system rather than a specific application. Moreover, all the above defense systems are implemented on x86 platform. Our work is focusing on the LLC-based attack and defense on both ARM architecture.

2.3.6 Recent Research on ARM-based Defenses

On the year 2017, Sandro Pinto and some other researchers proposed LTZVisor [41], which is based on TrustZone to protect and assist ARM virtualization. They implemented and tested on ARM platform and causing an overhead of around 22% at the highest user switching frequency. Guan el al. proposed TrustShadow [42], using TrustZone to protect user's applications, with little or no change on the application itself. The overhead here is around 10% at worst case and 2% on average. However, the framework is not tested on ARMv8-M, which has different structure and instruction sets from ARM Cortex-A series. Similar as LTZVisor, Hua et al. designed and implemented vTZ [43], a virtualization based defense framework on ARM. The overhead of vTZ is on average case around 5%.

According to their work, the most popular solution on ARM is virtualization, using TrustZone to protect the application, data and user's private keys. This can only be implemented on ARM Cortex-A series, which has different level of cache, multiple privilege levels and powerful CPU. On ARMv8-M series, however, similar implementation is not applicable. On ARMv8-M series chips, there is no cache on the structure, and normally the protection cannot be complicated due to the limited resource on the devices. Compared with their work, we have a more directly protection, with acceptable overhead and good performance.

2.4 Overview

2.4.1 Background

Environment Overview As multi-core processors become pervasive and the number of on-die cores increases, a key design issue facing processor architects is the hierarchy and policies for the on-die LLC. With LLC techniques, a CPU might only need to get around 5% data from main memory, which can improve the efficiency of CPU largely. On ARM, we are using Juno r1 Development Platform which has one A57 and one A53 processors on the board. A57 has a 2M LLC on the processor.

With the increasing complexity of computing systems, as well as multiple level of memory access, some registers are designed to store some specific hardware events. These registers are usually called hardware performance counters. We have many tools getting information from those performance counters, thus getting the performance information.

In our implementation, we cannot use perf for collecting timing information of memory access on ARM, since it cannot be accurate enough, and not applicable on ARM. On this chapter we use inline assemblies to measure time associated information with our side-channels.

Process Structures On implementations at ARM platform, the model contains with a sender, a receiver and an OS module to randomly inject cache flushes to generate noises into the channel. If the sender and the receiver are both from the attacker, it is a typical covert channel. If the sender program is a legitimate program, it is a typical side-channel configuration.

In this chapter, a channel is constructed and evaluated. The sender here sends a message in the stream. The receiver, on the other hand, analyzes the access time to the memory shared with the sender to figure out what is being sent. After receiver receiving the message, we study the quality of such channel in terms of bandwidth, accuracy with noises injections to the message channel.

We also have the error correction in the message channel. On this chapter, we use CRC for this purpose. The message passed through the message channel are checked using CRC, and when noises injected, the receiver uses CRC to try fixing the message, working to recover the message that the sender is sending.

Attack Based on ARM Platform Attacks using shared resource based side-channels need to monitor the victim's activities on the shared resource. Using cache as an example, in a Flush+Reload attack, the attacker firstly Flushes specific cache lines, and waits for a predetermined time to reload the contents. By measuring the reload time, the attacker can learn if the shared contents with the victim have been used or not, thus deriving sensitive information about the victim.

Similarly, in a Prime+Probe attack, the attacker first measures the data reading time, and loads memory contents (Prime) to a number of cache sets. The attacker then measures the access time to see if the data is accessed by the others (Probe). The success of such side-channel attacks is highly depending on the following three necessary conditions: (1) the ability to precisely measure the memory access time; (2) the ability to selectively manipulate cache contents; and (3) sharing memory contents with the victim.

On both x86 and ARM architecture, there are performance counter registers and related machine instructions to obtain accurate time measurement to satisfy condition (1). Condition (3) can be easily satisfied since a modern operating system has a lot of shared memory pages through the shared libraries, code segments, etc. The challenge is to satisfy condition (2) on ARM architecture because the instructions to manipulate cache contents are privileged instructions that are not available to the regular users. If a user is at a privileged level, side-channel attacks are unnecessary. Thus, ARM architecture is secure by design if a single operating system is running on the processor. However, these support on ARM may open the door to side-channel attacks due to handling of cache operations.

Background on Different Structures of ARM As mentioned above, on this book, we focus on ARM Cortex-A structure. However, devices and users using ARM Cortex-M structure are in a rising trend of numbers. On ARMv8-M, it does not have cache and memory mapping. Instead, it uses direct allocation on memory to ensure high performance. The memory on ARMv8-M is separated into different parts for different purposes.

As a result, the TrustZone entry and exit operations are with high efficiency, costing less than 10% of clock cycles comparing with Cortex-A series. On the other hand, the design of ARMv8-M made it difficult for design of defense. As devices using this structure usually with a simple or almost no OS, traditional defense framework are not applicable on those devices.

Based on our experiments and discussions, we can only focus on Cortex-A defense. For Cortex-M based defending framework, we focus on that topic on some other papers and publications.

2.4.2 Threat Model and Assumptions

Side-channel attackers and other cache-based attackers are not based on compromised OS. They perform as 'man in the middle' and collecting time stamps of cache read/write operations. As discussed above, for side-channel attack, the processes do not need shared memory, so the model here has no assumption that they have to share memory in whole or in part. Because of the difference in the definition between side-channel and covert channel, on covert channel, it is possible that the attacker and victim share some resources, making a slight difference on the assumption. In our design of defense, we can efficiently decrease the bandwidth of both side-channel and covert channel, but we are testing the defense using side-channel attack model, so we assume that the memory is not shared between victim process and the attacker.

On system side, we assume that the operating system components in TrustZone is not compromised so that the attackers are forced to use covert channels or side-channels without explicitly violating access control policies enforced by the operating system or other protection mechanisms. Besides that, we also assume the system is having a control part, i.e. handler to inject interference into possible side-channel. Some instructions using assembly code is privileged to higher level to launch, so we assume they have the privilege level to inject noise. On the other hand, we assume that the noise injection process is not compromised, so the injection of noise is just for the defense, not for other malicious using like probing the cache.

We also assume that the attacker has sufficient privilege to access the memory access time. This is also needed for the covert channel, and for the performance analysis of the covert channel. Time measurement is the key to launch most popular cache attacks, like Flush+Reload attack, Prime+Probe attack, etc. The attackers collect the time stamps and process them locally to retrieve information. To ensure accuracy, the attacker have the access to consult with several registers. It is possible because TrustZone is not trapping those instructions.

2.5 Design and Implementations

2.5.1 Design Features

On devices with ARM chips, security design can be quite different from the same case on Desktop or even mobile phones. We even have to think about the difference with traditional design on ARM utilizing TrustZone. In this part, we analyze our design features, challenges and show how our design fit for the new ARM devices.

According to our design goal, we need to make sure the security framework we design is flexible. It should be easy to port from device to device, despite the function or the use of each device. For example, if the secure handler we design and implement is porting from a smart home monitor to a series of smart vehicles, we have to ensure the manufacturer is doing as little as they wish to make the system fit in to the new environment. On Desktop and other PCs, it is relatively easier because of the standard OS and capsuled interfaces. However, on ARM devices, we get very little from the OS, so we have to implement the flexibility within our framework.

The next critical issue for the ARM devices is power consumption. With the consideration of that, we have to discuss the need of the presentence of TrustZone once again. Although doing every implementation in TrustZone is simple and easy, it is not the best energy-efficient solution sometimes. To this target, we try to use the privilege level of ARM to work like TrustZone and thus cut down the energy cost. Energy is not a serious problem in the devices like smart home devices and smart cars, as they can easily recharge. However, it is a problem in some other devices like outdoor devices and wear-on devices. This makes it another challenging part of our design and implementation. The paging difference is also a challenge to our work.

Given the design of the project, we do not depend on the Hypervisor mode of ARM structure, and not rely on TrustZone protections.

Overview of our design is shown at Figure 6. In this figure, we use 1 to 7 to indicate different steps of a side-channel attack and the defense we design against to it. For victim process, it has connections with ARM TrustZone, and TrustZone is trapping with special instructions. Step 1 and 2 indicate the entry and exit of TrustZone. When it exits from TrustZone, an attacker can utilize the cache to launch side-channel attack, i.e. Flush+Reload attack, shown as step 3. To effectively defend against the side-channel threat, we are using Flush injection to cut down the bandwidth of the side-channel. On step 4, the noise injector sends cache FLUSH request, and connect with system components in TrustZone on step 5. Some security components in TrustZone will FLUSH the cache as step 7, and send some performance parameters to the monitor in noise injector as step 6. After the whole loop, the monitor can decide whether the injector should send some other requests, based on some data collected. On the next section, we introduce the design of the monitor, which is shown at Figure 7.

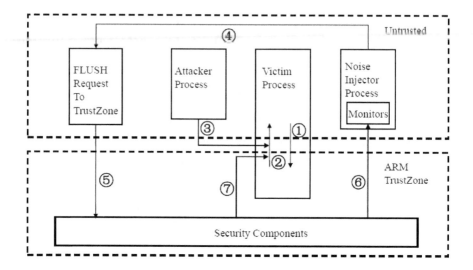

Figure 6: Defense Model Overview

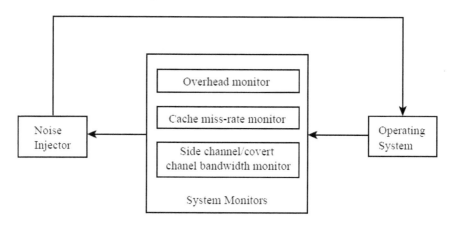

Figure 7: Adaptive Control Design with Monitor

2.5.2 Adaptive Control Model

Based on the design of defense model using FLUSH operations introduced above, we must find some balance between bandwidth elimination and performance overhead. As sometimes we need better performance and ignore minor bandwidth effects, we need to have some adaptive and flexible controlling methods to keep the balance of performance and security. As a result, we design a monitor between the noise injector and the OS. The designed architecture is shown on Figure 7.

For the monitor, we can set up different parameters of each category, and decide the FLUSH requests to the injector.

2.5.3 Implementations

In this section, we introduce some implementation details in the defense. On ARMv8 with TrustZone, the noise injector can send cache operation requests to TrustZone, and system components in TrustZone can handle them and trap the instructions. We control the frequency of trapping in FLUSH operations, and thus keeping a balance of security and performance.

For the structure we implement, the most critical parts are accurate time stamp collection, and cache FLUSH operation. For the non-secure world, as the users do not need to change their non-secure code, we do not need special care of them. For accurate time recording, it is needed for the analysis of bandwidth, and performance overhead. For cache FLUSH operation, it is the key to ensure the cache not going to be utilized by attackers.

Cache FLUSH Operations on ARM Platform. In order to add noises into the message channel, we consider having additional cache FLUSH operations. We use the third process to randomly add cache FLUSH operations, which do not target at some specific programs. As a result, these noise injections can be considered to protect the whole system. Implementing the FLUSH operation on x86 platform is straightforward using *clflush* instruction, but more complicated operations are on ARM platform for that.

As discussed above, on ARM, users have no access permission to cache FLUSH operations, as these operations are at privileged level. To better researching on the defense strategy on ARM, we build a message channel across the processes. However, on ARM platform, we do not have the instructions like *clflush* on x86 that are straightforward to deal with cache FLUSH operations. As a result, we have to take a look at the cache allocation on ARM, and use inline assembly codes to implement cache FLUSH operations.

It is usual to clean the cache before flushing it, so the external memory is updated with any dirty data. The following code segment shows how to clean and flush the entire cache.

```
MOV r0 , #0 ; Clear R0 ;
MCR p15 , 0 , r15 , c7 , c10 , 3 ;
// Flush DCache ;
```

On ARMv7 or higher, the cache FLUSH operations that are privileged and can be handled by ARM. In the code above, we can see the assembling code of flushing the cache uses MCR (Move to Coprocessor from Registers). The privileged operation using this can be trapped by the system, and system handles the operation referring to it. The reason is that, when an instruction uses MCR or MRC, the registers CP14 and CP15 are taken access. These registers are designed by ARM with special purpose, and used only for cache maintenance. For ARM, it has a system call which takes an array of those operations each specified by the struct called *mmuext_op*. This call allows access to various operations which must be performed with privileged level, like TLB operations, cache operations, and loading descriptor table base addresses.

Time Measurement on ARMv8. Unlike performance counters on x86, on ARMv8 platform, there are no instructions like perf to collect time-related performance counters from the system layer. Another challenge is that we cannot use rdtsc instruction to get time stamps as we often do on x86. Additionally, some other coarse-grained way like *gettimeofday()* certainly does not work.

Given these limitations, we have to be back to hardware, and look at ARM structure itself. We look up ARM whitebook and find some registers that we can retrieve time stamp information. However, when consulting with these registers, we have to enable them from kernel mode. By default, the access to these registers are disabled.

The following code segment shows the instructions for calculating time:

```
ISB ; MRS %0, cntvct_el 0 ;
// process execution ;
ISB ; MRS %0, cntvct_el 0 ;
ISB ; MRS %0, cntfrq_el 0 ;
```

We store the timestamps in two arrays and calculate the time based on these raw data. The instructions are privileged, and we can use timestamps for many monitor jobs. *cntfrq_el0* is used for reading current running frequency, which is not always the CPU frequency or clock frequency.

Other Implementations. Besides these, we also have other implementation features on this defense framework. We use Error Correction Code (ECC) to try recovering the contents missed due to quality loss. In this book we use CRC code to work as a checking and correcting process to try recovering the message that the sender just puts into the message channel. That is possible because the attacker may use some ECC to recover the data.

CRC is widely used in digital networks, and storage devices to detect abnormal data due to accidental changes to original data. At CRC, data are packed into blocks with a short check value attached, based on the remainder of a polynomial division of the contents of each block. CRC is popular in network applications because it is simple to implement, easy to analyze the data package from the check value, and good at detecting noise in message transmission channels.

However, CRC and other error correction codes have limitations. When we inject noise beyond a threshold, error correction may not work well, with some cases even performing worse and cannot correct the message according to the checksums. In our experiments, we add much noise into the message channel to defend against the attacker. As a result, CRC performs not well when the noise is injected for too much. It supports the noise injection mechanism for effective defense, as the attacker cannot even use ECC to recover original data.

We also implement a loop to control the frequency of FLUSH operations. The frequency is decided based on the performance monitor. Therefore, the total amount and frequency of noise injection are controlled in the protection side.

2.6 Evaluations

2.6.1 Experimental Setup and Metrics

In this chapter, we have different sets of experiments, testing the effectiveness of Flush-based adaptive defense. According to the experimental results, we have discussions on ARM Cortex-A series.

For Experiments, we target on two core problems: TrustZone and cache threats. For TrustZone experiments, we have experiments on following aspects:

- Percentage of TrustZone-related instructions;

- Cost of entering/exiting TrustZone;

- Effectiveness of TrustZone by bandwidth.

For cache threats, the major threat we focus on this chapter is side-channel attack. We have experiments on the following aspects:

- We FLUSH cache while exiting TrustZone and test the effectiveness;

- Cost of FLUSH operations;

- Effectiveness of FLUSH operations by bandwidth.

We also have theoretical discussions based on the experimental results. We have three aspects of theoretical analysis:

- We discuss bandwidth effect of FLUSH operations by theory;

- We discuss overhead effect of FLUSH operations by theory;

- We discuss defense performance by entropy.

For the first two aspects of discussion, we use curve regression to match the experimental results and theoretical discussions.

2.6.2 Experimental Results

We evaluate our proposed defense mechanisms using a proof-of-concept implementation on ARMv8 Platform. On ARM, we use a Juno r1 Development Platform, with one A57, one A53, the cache of L1 48KB for instruction, 32KB for data, and L2 for 2MB.

Cost of Interaction with ARM TrustZone. On ARM Cortex-A Platform, an instruction *smc* is used for connecting the secure world and non-secure world. While in normal non-secure world, some code could call privileged *smc* instruction. Then, secure world monitor will be triggered after validation. After execution of secure code, the return of the execution also calls *smc* to get back to the normal world. There are many open-source test platform to measure the world switch latency, and in this experiment, we use the well-known QEMU to test. It had been developed since the first patch published in 2011, and been patched by many manufacturers including Samsung, utilizing ARM TrustZone for security design.

For the experiments and results, we mention these on Chapter 1. As Table 1 and Table 2 shows, for different platform and different directions, ARM has different time costs. On ARM Cortex-A platform, the time costs of entry/exit are not small, in several thousands of clock cycles. However, due to the low usage of TrustZone communication, the total timing overhead could be acceptable. Note that the situation is only for current products without many uses of TrustZone; in the future, with the higher usage of TrustZone and communications between the secure world and outside system, the overhead can be a very tough problem to deal with.

Noise Injection to Flush+Reload based Side-Channels on ARMv8. As we described in Overview, on ARM platform with TrustZone protection, ARM can provide some protection for the cache against side-channel attack on the cache, using cache invalidation. However, it introduces significant performance loss. We revised implementation such that the amount of cache invalidation is under our control. Figure 8 shows the experimental results for a Flush+Reload based side-channel.

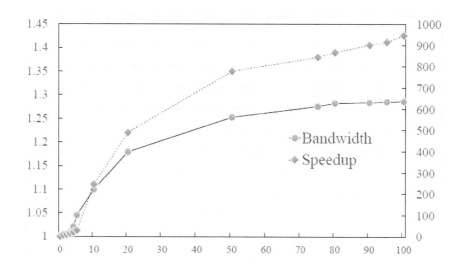

Figure 8: Bandwidth of a Flush+Reload based Side-Channel and Performance Improvement by Allowing a Specific Ratio of Cache Operations Passing through ARM Handling

In the figure, x-axis is the percentage of cache operations passing through the system handling. In other words, it is the percentage of cache operations that run on the processor hardware directly rather than being virtualized. Y-axis on the left is the performance speedup and y-axis on the right is the bandwidth of the side channel. If 0 percent cache operations passes through ARM handing, the bandwidth of the side-channel will be 0 and we set the corresponding execution time as the base value for the speedup measurement. When we have more cache operations passing through the ARM handling, we can get better performance on the execution. However, the bandwidth of the side-channel goes up as well. According to the experimental results, when we increase the percentage of cache operations passing through ARM handing, the bandwidth of potential side-channels in the whole platform will increase quickly up to 650 bits/second which is very practical and useful for side-channel attacks. At the same time, we can have performance improvement up to 43%. However, we do not want such kind of performance improvement due to the security risks of side-channel attacks. The trade-off must be chosen between a non-practical bandwidth of side-channel and acceptable performance improvement.

Noise Injection to Prime+Probe based Side-Channels on ARMv8. Similarly, when we inject flush operations to a system, it can also affect the bandwidth of Prime+Probe based side-channels. In our experiments, when we inject flush operations to incur about 20% overhead, the bandwidth of a side-channel can be decreased from about 600 bps to only several bps. The flush operations can effectively interfere with the time measurement in Prime+Probe based side-channels, thus making it non-practical.

Figure 9 shows the experimental results of noise injection into a Prime+Probe based side-channel. In the figure, x-axis is the percentage of cache operations passing through ARM handling. Y-axis on the left is the performance speedup and y-axis on the right is the bandwidth of the side-channel. The configuration of the experiment is the same as the Flush+Reload based side-channel except the type of side-channel is Prime+Probe. In the figure, we can see the different impact on speedup of the running of the program and bandwidth of side-channels caused by different percentage of passing-through cache operations from the injector process. When we pass-through more cache operations of a process (not trapped by the ARM platform and invalidate cache lines) we can see the speedup of an application increases, but also with increasing risks of side-channel attacks, as shown by fast increasing bandwidth of side-channels.

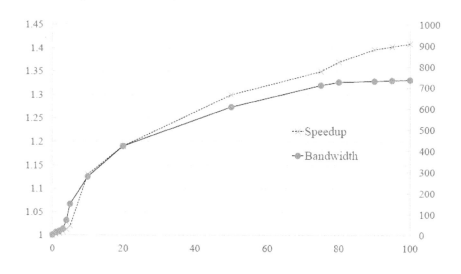

Figure 9: Bandwidth of Prime+Probe based Side-Channel and Performance Improvement by Allowing a Specific Ratio of Cache Operations Passing through ARM Handling

On ARM, as shown in Figure 9, when the ratio of not trapped cache operations increases to be about 10%, the bandwidth of side-channels quickly rises up to more than 200 bps, with speedup rising for only 13%. When the ratio increases to 75%, the bandwidth of side-channels rises up to more than 700 bps, with the speedup of application only by 35%. As a result, we can see that enabling ARM to pass-through some cache operations is not affordable, with very high risks of leaking information through side-channels. In other words, the way ARM handles the cache operations by processes is necessary to ensure security given the performance overheads. Otherwise, there will be greatly increased risks to have side-channel attacks on ARM platform.

2.7 Discussions

2.7.1 Theoretical Analysis

In this section, we describe theoretical analysis on the quality of the side-channels and also the impact of noise injections.

Information Theory based Analysis. The Shannon entropy [44] of a random variable $X: k \to \chi$ is defined in Equation (1).

$$H(X) = -\sum_{x \in \chi} p_X(x) \log_2 p_X(x) \quad (1)$$

The entropy is a lower bound of the average number of bits required for representing the results of independent repetitions of the experiment associated with X. In terms of our model, the entropy $H(X)$ is a lower bound of the effective information provided by one bit of the message.

Using our experimental results on ARM as an example, the accuracy at the receiver side with different level of noise injection is shown in Table 4. Note that we are using noise ratio as a parameter, which is a ratio of flush operations compared with all cache operations.

We use *srand()* to generate random numbers, so the distribution of the flush operations are of normal distribution. The entropy of the side channel has a relation with accuracy of the bits received through the side-channel. Thus, we calculate the entropy as follows.

$$H(X) = -\sum_{i=1}^{n} P(x_i)I(x_i) = -\sum_{i=1}^{n} P(x_i) \log_b P(x_i) \quad (2)$$

In our analysis, we set the value of b as 2 to calculate the entropy in bits. Now we consider multiple test cases. In each test, we use a ε to measure the percentage of noise injected in the test. Then, we calculate $H(X)$ and $H(Y)$, which are the entropy of the sender and the receiver respectively. As discussed before, the probability for the sender to send a 0 equals to the probability of sending a 1 for a random message.

39

Thus, we could use the following equations to calculate the quality of message channel with noise injected.

$$H(X) = - \sum_{i=1}^{n} P(x_i) \log_2 P(x_i) \qquad (3)$$

$$H(Y|X) = -\varepsilon \log_2 \varepsilon - (1 - \varepsilon) \log_2 (1 - \varepsilon) \qquad (4)$$

$$H(Y) = -- \sum_{i=1}^{n} (P(x_i) \log_2 P(x_i) + \varepsilon - 2\varepsilon P(x_i) \log_2 P(x_i)) \qquad (5)$$

Table 4: Overhead and Accuracy on ARM

Noise Ratio	Accuracy	Overhead (%)
0	0.918303	0
0.000010	0.790304	1
0.000100	0.685478	3
0.001000	0.596467	7
0.010000	0.526785	15
0.100000	0.513214	25
0.500000	0.495521	30

And we have the results with different noise injections ε, as shown in Table 5.

Table 5: Entropy and Noise Ratio

Noise Ratio	Accuracy	Entropy (H(x))
0	0.918303	0.4079
0.000010	0.790304	0.7409
0.000100	0.685478	0.8983
0.001000	0.596467	0.9728
0.010000	0.526785	0.9979
0.100000	0.513214	0.9995
0.500000	0.495521	0.9999

In the table, with a relatively high amount noise added into the side-channels, the entropy rises up quickly. It is close to the max value of 1 with around 50% operations added. When we add more noise, it makes the receiver harder to guess a bit from the sender. Therefore, when we have a probability close to 0.5 to fail, the entropy will have the highest value of 1.

Channel Quality. With different level of noise injection, a side-channel constructed by an attacker can be from highly risky to almost non-threatening. As discussed above, with the random injection of flush operations, the values of message entropy, the bandwidth and overhead are changed accordingly, as shown in Table 6.

Noise Ratio	Overhead (%)	Entropy	Bandwidth (bps)
0	0	0.4079	675
0.000010	1	0.7409	552
0.000100	3	0.8983	449
0.001000	7	0.9728	251
0.010000	15	0.9979	137
0.100000	25	0.9995	95
0.500000	30	0.9999	6

In the table, with the noise injected, both message entropy and overhead increase, while the bandwidth of side-channels decreases quickly. With more noise injected into the channel, it makes the channel filled in with additional noise, the entropy value increases.

As shown by Shannon entropy definition, when the entropy is close to 1, the message channel can be considered as very poor quality. For each bit with two possible values, the expected time of guesses for getting the correct bit is close to 2, which is nearly a situation with random guessing. If we have such kind of message channel, it cannot send meaningful message because of the difficulty for the receiver to get the corresponding bits.

However, the injected noises also have some negative impact on the system, which is shown as overhead in our experiments. There is a tradeoff between performance sacrifice and increasing of security. On ARM platform, we can achieve effective defense using flush operations injected into the system, with the performance overhead of about 20%, to effectively defend against the side-channel.

Statistical Discussion. Now we consider the bandwidth of side-channels in Figure 8 again. In the experiments where we randomly insert flush operations to interfere with the side-channels, the time of injecting noise is randomly distributed. Also, the interval of each pair of operations is randomly distributed. Exponential distribution is usually used to describe the distribution of intervals of a set of statistically independent events. In our experiment, we use it to describe the distribution of injected flush operations intervals. Every time the system flushes the cache, it affects the time measurement of the side-channel attacks. Thus, the bandwidth of possible side-channels is cut down. As a result, the flush operations can affect the bandwidth of side-channels, in the way of an exponential distribution.

When we look at the side-channel bandwidth, another factor we have to consider is the background noise from other running processes in the system. We model the system background noise using a uniform distribution. Therefore, the cumulative distribution function is as follows:

$$F(x, \lambda) = \begin{cases} 1 - e^{-\lambda x} & x \geq 0 \\ 0 & x < 0 \end{cases} \qquad (6)$$

Where λ is the rate parameter of exponential distribution. As we focus on the bandwidth with given ratio of passing-through cache operations, there cannot be the situation where x is less than 0. As mentioned above, we have to take the background noise into consideration. Thus, we have the function with more parameters as follows:

$$F(x, \lambda) = a(1 - e^{-\lambda x}) + b \qquad (7)$$

Where a is the maximum possible bandwidth under our experimental environments and b is the parameters of background noise.

Based on our experimental results and the above statistical analysis, we have a curve fitting function shown in Figure 10.

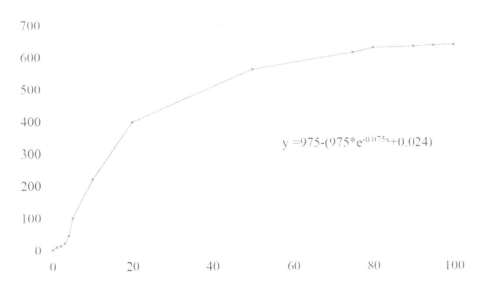

Figure 10: A Function for Side-Channel Bandwidth Prediction Based on Statistic Model

The function with parameters determined by experimental results is as follows.

$$F(x) = 975 - (975 * e^{-0.075x}) + 0.024 \qquad (8)$$

The function is used as a reference for adaptive noise injection and side-channel bandwidth prediction in the defense.

2.7.2 Adaptive Noise Injection

In the defense against the side-channels, we consider three critical system parameters: performance overhead, bandwidth of the possible side-channel, and the cache miss-rate. In our design, when the performance overhead is over a given threshold, or the cache miss rate is over a pre-determined threshold, noise injection will be stopped to maintain an acceptable performance. However, when the bandwidth of possible side-channels is high enough at a risky level, noise injection will be enabled to protect the system against side-channels.

We have conducted two sets of experiments to compare adaptive noise injection with simple random noise injection. In each set of the experiments, we compare the

43

overhead of the system or the bandwidth of the side-channels. In the first set of experiments, we control the cache miss-rate and performance overhead, and see the bandwidth differences between defense with and without the adaptive mechanism. In the second sets of experiments, we control the bandwidth and cache miss-rate, and compare the performance overhead between defense with and without adaptive mechanism. The experimental results are shown in Figure 11 and Figure 12.

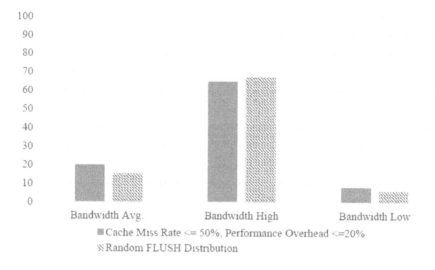

Figure 11: Side-Channel Bandwidth (bps) with and without Adaptive Mechanism

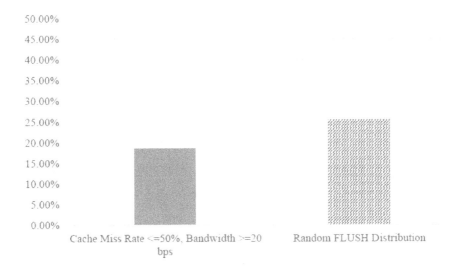

50.00%	
45.00%	
40.00%	
35.00%	
30.00%	
25.00%	
20.00%	
15.00%	
10.00%	
5.00%	
0.00%	

Cache Miss Rate <=50%, Bandwidth >=20 bps   Random FLUSH Distribution

Figure 12: Performance Overhead with and without Adaptive Mechanism

In Figure 11, the column on the left shows the experimental results for the adaptive defense. We set up the threshold of cache miss rate to 50%, the performance overhead to 20% and bandwidth to 20 bps. When the cache miss rate is less than 50%, and the performance overhead is less than 20%, we add cache flush operations to interfere with the side-channels.

According to the experimental results, when adaptive noise injection is used, the average bandwidth of the side-channels can be similar. However, we can obtain better performance while dealing with high bandwidth situations. When the cache miss-rate is relatively low and performance overhead is low, the risk of leaking information through shared resources is relatively higher. When we target at this situation and inject more noises to the system, the interference can be effective. On the other hand, when the performance overhead is high and the cache miss-rate is also high, frequent cache flush operations provide a very tough situation for cache based side-channel attacks. Under such circumstance, there is little need to inject more cache operations as noises.

Figure 12, on the other hand, shows the results of the second set of experiments. In this set of experiments, we mainly consider the performance overhead of the defending strategy. Without adaptive noise injection, the overhead is always as high as 20%-30%. However, as some of the cache flush operations are not necessary, our adaptive noise injection can avoid a great amount of flush operations when they are not needed. As a result, when we set the noise injection threshold to the cache miss-rate of 50% and bandwidth of over 20 bps, the overhead average can be optimized to less than 20%, to be about 18.5%.

According to experiments above, when we set up a monitor and control the parameters according to our need, we can have better performance without too much loss on the system's cache miss rate, overhead or security concerns. For further defense design, we can have different parameters fitting into the monitor, and the user can decide which parameters they care most. As a result, the monitor can make the defense adaptive, flexible, and also portable.

2.8 Chapter Conclusions

It has been proved that in the side-channel attacks, the attacker can steal users' private information even if the operating system is not compromised. To counter this growing threat, we present a new software-only defense mechanism to mitigate the LLC based side-channel attack. Our defense randomly flushes the cache to inject noise in FLUSH+RELOAD. We qualify our defense mechanism using Shannon entropy analysis. We implement the proposed defense on ARM V8 architecture. The experimental results show that with less than 5% system performance overhead, our approach effectively lowers the accuracy of the side-channel to around 70%. We also introduce an adaptive monitor to balance the efficiency, security concerns and performance overhead. The results show that cache flushing with adaptive strategy can effectively reduce the threats of side-channel attack, and the user can still control the defense based on their own needs.

In future work, we will investigate the ARM instructions to further reduce the overhead of current defense. We also plan to port the monitor to ARMv8-M platform. We will design and implement a defense framework for ARMv8 platform, both for ARMv8-A and ARMv8-M series. If we can implement the defense framework, we will provide a better environment for the users and developers. It will be a good protection for IoT network.

References

[1] Yarom, Y. and Falkner, K. (2014) FLUSH+RELOAD: A High Resolution, Low Noise, L3 Cache Side-Channel Attack. In 23rd USENIX Security Symposium (USENIX Security 14) (San Diego, CA: USENIX Association): 719–732. URL https://www.usenix.org/conference/usenixsecurity14/technical-sessions/presentation/yarom.

[2] Irazoqui, G., Inci, M.S., Eisenbarth, T. and Sunar, B. (2014) Wait a Minute! A fast, Cross-VM Attack on AES (Cham: Springer International Publishing), 299–319. doi:10.1007/978-3-319-11379-1_15, URL http://dx.doi.org/10.1007/978-3-319-11379-1_15.

[3] Zhang, Y., Juels, A., Reiter, M.K. and Ristenpart, T. (2014) Cross-tenant side-channel attacks in paas clouds. In Proceedings of the 2014 ACM SIGSAC Conference on Computer and Communications Security, CCS '14 (New York, NY, USA: ACM): 990–1003.doi:10.1145/2660267.2660356, URL http://doi.acm.org/10.1145/2660267.2660356.

[4] Gülmezoglu, B., Inci, M.S., Irazoqui, G., Eisenbarth, T. and Sunar, B. (2015) A Faster and More Realistic Flush+Reload Attack on AES (Cham: Springer International Publishing), 111–126. doi:10.1007/978-3-319-21476-4_8, URL http://dx.doi.org/10.1007/978-3-319-21476-4_8.

[5] Santos, N., Raj, H., Saroiu, S. and Wolman, A. (2014) Using arm trustzone to build a trusted language runtime for mobile applications. In Proceedings of the 19th International Conference on Architectural Support for Programming Languages and Operating Systems, ASPLOS '14 (New York, NY, USA: ACM): 67–80.

doi:10.1145/2541940.2541949, URL http://doi.acm.org/10.1145/2541940.2541949.

[6] Azab, A.M., Ning, P., Shah, J., Chen, Q., Bhutkar, R., Ganesh, G., Ma, J. et al. (2014) Hypervision across worlds: Real-time kernel protection from the arm trustzone secure

world. In Proceedings of the 2014 ACM SIGSAC Conference on Computer and Communications Security (ACM): 90–102.

[7] Kwon, D., Oh, K., Park, J., Yang, S., Cho, Y., Kang, B.B. and Paek, Y. (2018) Hypernel: a hardware-assisted framework for kernel protection without nested paging. In Proceedings of the 55th Annual Design Automation Conference (ACM): 34.

[8] Frenzel, T., Lackorzynski, A., Warg, A. and Härtig, H. (2010) Arm trustzone as a virtualization technique in embedded systems. In Proceedings of Twelfth Real-Time Linux Workshop, Nairobi, Kenya: 29–42.

[9] Lipp, M., Gruss, D., Spreitzer, R., Maurice, C. and Mangard, S. (2016) Armageddon: Cache attacks on mobile devices. In USENIX Security Symposium: 549–564.

[10] Bernstein, D.J. (2005) Cache-timing attacks on AES. Tech. rep.

[11] Page, D. (2005), Partitioned cache architecture as a side-channel defence mechanism. URL http://eprint.iacr.org/2005/280. Page@cs.bris.ac.uk 13017 received 22 Aug 2005.

[12] Wang, Z. and Lee, R.B. (2007) New cache designs for thwarting software cache-based side channel attacks. In Proceedings of the 34th Annual International Symposium on Computer Architecture, ISCA '07: 494–505.

[13] Wang, Z. and Lee, R.B. (2008) A novel cache architecture with enhanced performance and security. In 2008 41st IEEE/ACM International Symposium on Microarchitecture: 83–93. doi:10.1109/MICRO.2008.4771781.

[14] Liu, F. and Lee, R.B. (2014) Random fill cache architecture. In 2014 47th Annual IEEE/ACM International Symposium on Microarchitecture: 203–215. doi:10.1109/MICRO.2014.28.

[15] Brickell, E., Graunke, G., Neve, M. and Seifert, J.P. (2006), Software mitigations to hedge aes against cache-based software side channel vulnerabilities.

[16] Cleemput, J.V., Coppens, B. and De Sutter, B. (2012) Compiler mitigations for time attacks on modern x86 processors. ACM Trans. Archit. Code Optim. 8(4): 23:1–23:20. doi:10.1145/2086696.2086702, URL http://doi.acm.org/10.1145/2086696.2086702.

[17] Crane, S., Homescu, A., Brunthaler, S., Larsen, P. and Franz, M. (2015) Thwarting cache side-channel attacks through dynamic software diversity. In 22nd Annual Network and Distributed System Security Symposium, NDSS 2015, San Diego, California, USA, February 8-11, 2014.

[18] Tromer, E., Osvik, D.A. and Shamir, A. (2010) Efficient cache attacks on aes, and countermeasures. Journal of Cryptology 23(1): 37–71. Doi: 10.1007/s00145-009-9049-y, URL http://dx.doi.org/10.1007/s00145-009-9049-y.

[19] Liu, F., Yarom, Y., Ge, Q., Heiser, G. and Lee, R.B. (2015) Last-level cache side channel attacks are practical. In 2015 IEEE Symposium on Security and Privacy: 605-622. doi:10.1109/SP.2015.43.

[20] Page, D. (2003) Defending against cache based side-channel attacks. Information Security Technical Report 8(1): 30–44.

[21] Zhang, Y. and Reiter, M.K. (2013) Düppel: retrofitting commodity operating systems to mitigate cache side-channels in the cloud. In Proceedings of the 2013 ACM SIGSAC conference on Computer & Communications security, CCS '13 (New York, NY, USA: ACM): 827–838. doi:10.1145/2508859.2516741, URL http://doi.acm.org/10.1145/2508859.2516741.

[22] Varadarajan, V., Ristenpart, T. and Swift, M. (2014) Scheduler-based defenses against cross-vm side-channels. In 23rd USENIX Security Symposium (USENIX Security 14) (San Diego, CA: USENIX Association): 687–702. URL https://www.usenix.org/conference/usenixsecurity14/technical-sessions/presentation/varadarajan.

[23] Crane, S., Homescu, A., Brunthaler, S., Larsen, P. and Franz, M. (2015) Thwarting cache side-channel attacks through dynamic software diversity. In NDSS: 8–11.

[24] Liu, F., Ge, Q., Yarom, Y., Mckeen, F., Rozas, C., Heiser, G. and Lee, R.B. (2016) Catalyst: Defeating last-level cache side channel attacks in cloud computing. In High Performance Computer Architecture (HPCA), 2016 IEEE International Symposium on (IEEE): 406–418.

[25] Chen, S., Zhang, X., Reiter, M.K. and Zhang, Y. (2017) Detecting privileged side-channel attacks in shielded execution with déjà vu. In Proceedings of the 2017 ACM on Asia Conference on Computer and Communications Security (ACM): 7–18.

[26] Ristenpart, T., Tromer, E., Shacham, H. and Savage, S. (2009) Hey, you, get off of my cloud: exploring information leakage in third-party compute clouds. In Proceedings of the 16th ACM conference on Computer and communications security, CCS '09 (New York, NY, USA: ACM): 199–212. doi:10.1145/1653662.1653687, URL http://doi.acm.org/10.1145/1653662.1653687.

[27] Xu, Y., Bailey, M., Jahanian, F., Joshi, K., Hiltunen, M. and Schlichting, R. (2011) An exploration of l2 cache covert channels in virtualized environments. In Proceedings of the 3rd ACM Workshop on Cloud Computing Security Workshop, CCSW '11 (New York, NY, USA: ACM): 29–40. doi:10.1145/2046660.2046670, URL http://doi.acm.org/10.1145/2046660.2046670.

[28] Percival, C. (2005) Cache missing for fun and profit. In Proc. of BSDCan 2005.

[29] Wu, Z., Xu, Z. and Wang, H. (2015) Whispers in the hyper-space: High-bandwidth and reliable covert-channel attacks inside the cloud. IEEE/ACM Trans. Netw. 23(2): 603–614. doi:10.1109/TNET.2014.2304439, URL http://dx.doi.org/10.1109/TNET.2014.2304439.

[30] Zhang, Y., Juels, A., Oprea, A. and Reiter, M.K. (2011) Homealone: Co-residency detection in the cloud via side-channel analysis. In Proceedings of the 2011 IEEE

Symposium on Security and Privacy, SP '11 (Washington, DC, USA: IEEE Computer Society): 313–328. doi:10.1109/SP.2011.31, URL http://dx.doi.org/10.1109/SP.2011.31.

[31] Gullasch, D., Bangerter, E. and Krenn, S. (2011) Cache games – bringing access-based cache attacks on aes to practice. In Proceedings of the 2011 IEEE Symposium on Security and Privacy, SP '11 (Washington, DC, USA: IEEE Computer Society): 490–505. doi:10.1109/SP.2011.22, URL http://dx.doi.org/10.1109/SP.2011.22.

[32] Irazoqui, G., Eisenbarth, T. and Sunar, B. (2015) S$a: A shared cache attack that works across cores and defies vm sandboxing – and its application to aes. In The proceedings of 2015 IEEE Symposium on Security and Privacy (San Jose, CA: IEEE): 591–604.

[33] Shih, M.W., Lee, S., Kim, T. and Peinado, M. (2017) T-sgx: Eradicating controlled-channel attacks against enclave programs. In Proceedings of the 2017 Annual Network and Distributed System Security Symposium (NDSS), San Diego, CA.

[34] Moghimi, A., Irazoqui, G. and Eisenbarth, T. (2017) Cachezoom: How sgx amplifies the power of cache attacks. arXiv preprint arXiv:1703.06986 .

[35] Xu, Y., Cui, W. and Peinado, M. (2015) Controlled-channel for untrusted operating systems. In 2015 IEEE Symposium on Security and Privacy: 640–656. doi:10.1109/SP.2015.45.

[36] Chen, X., Garfinkel, T., Lewis, E.C., Subrahmanyam, P., Waldspurger, C.A., Boneh, D., Dwoskin, J. et al. (2008) Overshadow: A virtualization-based approach to retrofitting protection in commodity operating systems. In In ASPLOS.

[37] Hofmann, O.S., Kim, S., Dunn, A.M., Lee, M.Z. and Witchel, E. (2013) Inktag: Secure applications on an untrusted operating system. In ASPLOS'13, 2013 (New York, NY, USA: ACM): 265–278. doi:10.1145/2451116.2451146, URL http://doi.acm.org/10.1145/2451116.2451146.

[38] Baumann, A., Peinado, M. and Hunt, G. (2014) Shielding applications from an untrusted cloud with haven. In OSDI'14, 2014 (Broomfield, CO: USENIX Association): 267–283. URL https://www.usenix.org/conference/osdi14/technical-sessions/presentation/baumann.

[39] Zhou, Z., Reiter, M.K. and Zhang, Y. (2016), A software approach to defeating side channels in last-level caches, arXiv preprint, arXiv: 1603.05615v1. http://arxiv.org//.

[40] Zhang, N., Sun, K., Lou, W. and Hou, T. (2016) Case: Cache-assisted secure execution on arm processors. In The 37th IEEE Symposium on Security and Privacy (S&P) (SAN JOSE, CA: IEEE).

[41] Pinto, S., Pereira, J., Gomes, T., Tavares, A. and Cabral, J. (2017) Ltzvisor: Trustzone is the key. In LIPIcs-Leibniz International Proceedings in Informatics (Schloss Dagstuhl-Leibniz-Zentrum fuer Informatik), 76.

[42] Guan, L., Liu, P., Xing, X., Ge, X., Zhang, S., Yu, M. and Jaeger, T. (2017) Trustshadow: Secure execution of unmodified applications with arm trustzone. In Proceedings of the 15th Annual International Conference on Mobile Systems, Applications, and Services (ACM): 488–501.

[43] Hua, Z., Gu, J., Xia, Y., Chen, H., Zang, B. and Guan, H. (2017) vtz: Virtualizing arm trustzone. In In Proc. of the 26th USENIX Security Symposium.

[44] Shannon, C.E. (2001) A mathematical theory of communication. SIGMOBILE Mob. Comput. Commun. Rev. 5(1): 3–55. doi:10.1145/584091.584093, URL http://doi.acm.org/10.1145/584091.584093.

Publisher: Eliva Press SRL

Email: info@elivapress.com

Eliva Press is an independent publishing house established for the publication and dissemination of academic works all over the world. Company provides high quality and professional service for all of our authors.

Our Services:
Free of charge, open-minded, eco-friendly, innovational.

-All services are free of charge for you as our author (manuscript review, step-by-step book preparation, publication, distribution, and marketing).
-No financial risk. The author is not obliged to pay any hidden fees for publication.
-Editors. Dedicated editors will assist step by step through the projects.
-Money paid to the author for every book sold. Up to 50% royalties guaranteed.
-ISBN (International Standard Book Number). We assign a unique ISBN to every Eliva Press book.
-Digital archive storage. Books will be available online for a long time. We don't need to have a stock of our titles. No unsold copies. Eliva Press uses environment friendly print on demand technology that limits the needs of publishing business. We care about environment and share these principles with our customers.
-Cover design. Cover art is designed by a professional designer.
-Worldwide distribution. We continue expanding our distribution channels to make sure that all readers have access to our books.

www.elivapress.com

www.ingramcontent.com/pod-product-compliance
Lightning Source LLC
LaVergne TN
LVHW052314060326
832902LV00021B/3890